Learn How To Plan Your Hotel Business

Potential income from 500k and above..

<Your Company>

YOUR HOTEL BUSINESS PLAN

Table of Contents

1. Learn How To Create Company Profile

- Company Profile

- Business License

- Business Owner Background

  (Attach your company profile here)

2.   What You Should Write in Project Executive Summary

A. Project Brief

This document is being prepared for the establishment of high quality hotel in *(Type in your home town)*. The objective to establish the hotel is to facilitate the internal and external tourist by providing them with the best boarding and lodging facilities.

The hotel will provide accommodation facilities for *(how many guest / rooms)*. Apart from the usual guest entertainment, we also have event facilities, café, bistro, restaurant, transport and touring services available to non-occupants. The competitive advantage of the current project would be its prime location and provision of excellent and competitive services to occupants and non-occupants.

The project is proposed to be located at *(Type in your business address here)*. *(Type in the famous place at your area, population of the city or town and public facilities that is available in the city or town)* Example: The city has been listed as a UNESCO World Heritage Site since 7 July 2016, with population of 872,900 peoples on year 2015 and covers an area of 1,664 km2 (642 sq mi). Malacca is considered a gate way for all the tourist activities of the locality. The region has access all the public amenities including water, electricity, public transport and telecommunication facilities.

The completion time for the project is *(How long is the project to be completed)*. **The capital cost is** *(How much is the cost needed to implement the project)* **while the initial working capital required would be** *(How much is your working capital)*, **thus the total cost would be** *(The overall project cost)*. The Sale at 60% occupancy i.e. *(total hotel rooms)* rooms and allied services is *(estimated revenue)* per year. The human resource requirement is *(how many person)* personal in the managerial, skilled and semi-skilled level. There will also be numerous jobs created indirectly. There is no problem of entry into the market as the people here are known to be very friendly and there are no monopolies in this area of the economy.

B. Financial Summary

- *Fill-in the financial summary*

Financial Summary

No.	Descriptions	Total Amount (RM) / Percentage (%)
1	Sales	
2	Gross Profit Margin	
3	Net Profit Margin	
4	Internal Rate of Return	
5	NPV @ 10%	
6	Pay Back Period (Years)	

Chart 1: Financial Summary

3.   Learn How To Do Your Market Research & Analysis

I.   ABC Hotel's Product Mix

Accommodation

The accommodation of *(Your Company)* consists of various suites (honeymoon, deluxe, business) and rooms (single and double rooms). Each room includes a bathroom, TV mini bar, air-conditioner, and internet access. Several rooms will have panoramic view while most have a garden historical view. Additionally *(Your Company)* will offer security coded entrance to building and rooms, safety deposit boxes, secure luggage storage, 24/7 reception and helpdesk and business amenities. *(You may also need to state the actual accommodation that your hotel offer to the customer)*

Food Service / Room Service/ Cafe' & Restaurant

Food service is intended to serve a complementary breakfast. Room service will offer lunch and dinner to guests, but also will cater to convention customers during meetings. Due to the nature of our hotel, we will serve healthy foods, and can even provide a special diet service. *(You may also need to state the actual service that your hotel offer to the customer)*

Recreation

(Your Company) also offer access to activities in the surrounding area. We are offering on the amenities as can expected of the location. Amenities available within the immediate area: Walking, bicycling, boating, tours of the city, and many more within your *(city/hotel)*.

Mini Shop *(if any, you can add-in)*

Your Company will also very convenience for our hotel customer and local area to shop on household products, stationary, light foods and drinks.

Conference Facilities

(Your Company) will have *(total unit of your conference room)* conference room, which can be used for meetings, seminar, parties and corporate gathering.

The product line offers the following additional advantages:

I. **For families** – For families we offer special discount for accommodations, meals, laundry, and tour packages. *(Sample)*

II. **For business travelers** – For business travelers we have a complete range of conference and business facilities such as office space, fax, printer and secretarial services and broad band internet connections. Our meeting rooms are fully equipped for conferences and we have transportation services to and from the hotel to the airport and major historical area within *(your hotel/city)*. *(Sample)*

III. **For couples without children** – For tourist couples without children we have a large variety of amenities catering to the young and old such as a full program of recreational activities: walking, bicycling, boating and historical tours of *(your city name)* areas and many more. *(Sample)*

IV. **For single and group travel** – For the single or group traveler there is a selection of group activities available which can be reserved in advance or after arrival at the hotel. These activities include sports and recreation, dinner, guided tours and organised coach travel to areas of interest in the region. All group travel can be accompanied by a guide and the hotel can handle any in-house catering for groups. *(Sample)*

V. **For physically impaired** – The hotel is amply suitable and adapted to persons who travel in wheelchairs, need nursing care, have vision or hearing difficulties or otherwise require easy access to amenities, services and accommodation. All hotel building are low on thresholds. Ramps and elevators are located where stairs are necessary, there is clear signing of all services and amenities and rooms can be fitted out with alarm buttons for immediate medical attention. *(Sample)*

II. **Market Analysis**

At *(Your Company)*, the following tools were used to analyze and to explore the market:

   a. Inquiries with existing and potential customers
   b. Requested information from community business support groups
   c. Collected catalogues, price list and brochures of competitors
   (You may also can put in your ideas on the market analysis tools if any)

The hospitality or hotel market is good business for *(your city name)* which the town is the most historical and have the ability to attract a lot of tourists come over as per following trending and several assessment factors:

➤ Target Trend

- *Write a history about your city/town historical / interesting place in your city/town.*

- *Write a bit about your city/town location.*

- *Do a bit research about your area size, what are other city/town within your area and write also any local/international recognition about the area.*

- *What is the language used / have in your city/town.*

- *Describe a bit about your area development or current economy.*

(Do a research on this part)

➢ Market Target

(City/Town) has an estimated **population of** *(total population, example: 900,000)* **as of** *(which year)* with an average annual population growth of *(growth percentage example 10%)* as of *(which year), (percentage of age example: 25% of the population aged below 15 years old and 7% aged above 60 years old). (Explain about ethnicity within your target market example: The ethnic composition of Malacca is Malays (63%), Chinese and Peranakan (25.3%), Indians and Chitty (6%) and the minority Kristang, Dutch Eurasian and Temuan community).*

(List out all the interest place within your market that which can attract tourist and local to visit the area)

➢ Assessment of Project Site

The sample results of the assessment of the project site are summarized as follows:

Criteria	Assessment				
	--	-	0	+	++
Visibility					√
Accessibility by car					√
Accessibility by means of public transport				√	
General transportation coverage					√
image					√
View from hotel				√	
Quality / appearance of sorroundings					√
Environmental situation					√
Security					√
Cleanliness					√
Tourist attractiveness					√
Shopping facilities in the vicinity					√
High-end gastronomic facilities in the vacinity					√
Entertainment facility in the vicinity					√

Chart 2: Assessment of Project Site

➢ Hotel Matrix

The following are sample of hotel matrix illustrates the suitability of the location "**Your Company**" for each category.

Hotel Type		Suitability of Melaka Site for particular hotel type				
Type	Category	--	-	0	+	++
City Hotel	Five star (luxury)					√
	Four stars (upper class)				√	
	Three stars (economy)		√			
	Two stars (budget)	√				
	One star (low budget)	√				
Motel	N/A	√				
Holiday resort	N/A	√				
Service apartments	N/A				√	
All suites hotel	N/A				√	

Chart 3: Hotel Matrix

➢ Guest Matrix

The following is sample of guest matrix shows the assessment of the suitability of the project site for the different types of hotels, related to guest segmentation. Moreover, with an excellent visibility and accessibility this hotel project undoubtedly will benefit from having by far the best location.

Gust Segment		Suitability of hotel site for demand by particular by particular guest				
Purpose of travel	Category	--	-	0	+	++
Business	Business traveler				√	√
	Fair / Congress attendees				√	
	Conference/Seminar attendees				√	
Leisure	Individual tourists					√
	Group tourists					√
	Weddings					√
Miscellaneous	Long-stay guests				√	

Chart 4: Guest Matrix

➤ Market Share / **Regional analysis**

The size of the market in the region averages anywhere from 50-90% occupancy rate throughout the year. **Your Company** intends to capture a portion of this regional market. This market has experienced erratic growth in the past few years related to the national economy. Budget and luxury hotel in the area average 110 rooms *(put in your own figure that you have analyzed)* and rooms rates of USD 250.00 to USD350.00 **(put rates of hotel based on your analysis). ABC Company** will capture a portion of **(how many percentages of your market portion that you think, example 5%)** of tourists that yearly visits the area.

➤ Market Share objectives

The number of direct competitor is estimated at 0. This is because **Your Company** will offer convention facilities that are unmatch in the region with size and pricing.

➤ Market Segmentation

Four type of hotel properties generally appeal to leisure travelers: economy, mid-priced, upscale and premium budget hotels & resorts. Because of its location and formula the hotel will cater primarily to business people and will be open all year.

> ➢ Customer profile (sample)

Product	Business guests	Tourists	Area	Other
accommodation	X	X	X	
Restaurants & cafe	X	X	X	
Conference rooms	X		X	
Parties & catering	X	X	X	X
recreation		X	X	X
Mini Shop	X	X	X	

Chart 5: Customer Profile

In general the purpose of visit will be 75% tourism, 5% family visit, and 20% is business related. (key-in your on visitor percentage based in your research or your can get from your local authority)

III.   **Marketing goals**

An important part of *Your Company's* marketing goals and strategies will be establish and maintain its level of quality accommodation and associated service. To this end we will regularly invite representatives of the various ratings to visit the Your Company to ensure that we will remain listed within the best quality hotel in *(key-in your town/city name here)*. Upgrades and renovations will be carried out whenever necessary.

In our marketing goals, we also taking care on our personnel and the marketing concept. The employees must be able to carry out the philosophy and the strategy of the company. This will be emphasized until the strategies are carried out as planned and the results are obvious. All new strategies will be forwarded and discuss with the employees on a regular basis during the weekly meetings. Responsible for the correct flow of information will be the department heads as laid out in the organizational chart. *(You can add-in and modify using your own word that is more valuable or suitable to your business)*

IV.   **Pricing strategy**

In the hotel market, there is an overall tendency to consider the competitive offers as well as the degree of acceptance by the customers when planning a pricing strategy. *Your Company* will follow this tendency.

Your Company's services are priced at parity with or at a slight premium over competitive offerings. Extensive promotional activity, including daily and holiday specials, help to ensure that customers perceive that they are receiving higher quality products and prompt, courteous service in exchange for the slight premium in price.

For *Your Company*'s Mini Shop, Cafe,Restaurant, the price will be consider according to current market price. Extensive promotional activity also will be planned for the offer, example like various discount, offer and etc.

(You can add-in and modify using your own word that is more valuable or suitable to your business)

V. Operations

Classical cum Modern Identity / Premium Budget Hotel

Your Company and classical cum modern identity will be made clear by its furnishings and decoration and for its focus on job skills training. Its classical cum modern style will be reflected in the buildings, grounds, accommodation and all amenities and facilities the hotel offers.

Hotel Location

The operation location is located in **(key-in your town/city)**. This location has been selected because of the location is very strategic, visibility and image. The location will also provide our employees as well as our customers with the necessary accessibility. We are open for business throughout the year being located in full season climate.

Location Overview

Location	Description
Immediate area	
Type of area	Historical area, business area
Adjacent uses	Entertainment, Touring, Shopping
Benefits	Busy area throughout the year
Proximity	
Customer type	Tourists, business travelers, family visit
Potential customers	Local up through international guests
Competitors	Many hotel but only one with great place & offer
Traffic volume	
Patterns	Large intersection nearby
Situation	Easy access to main road
Pedestrians	Low pedestrian area
Periods	Between 6.00am-9.00am, 12.00pm-2.00pm, 4.30pm-6.30pm is extremely busy with nearby school, working hours and public holidays.
Accessibility	
Close to major streets	Near river, shopping area and historical area
Easy entrance/exit	Open doors, easy to walk in
Visibility	
From road	Easy to see, signs with logo will be visible
Appear of exterior	New construction
Landscaping	Lanscaping area surrounding the hotel

Chart 6: Sample Location Overview

Outside City Limits

The location of the hotel has been chosen because of the charm of the natural surroundings, the accessibility to existing infrastructure such as the airport, bus station, railway and the national highway grid. The remoteness of the location offers an ideal retreat for tourist and business travelers who seek a place away from urban areas and the hustle and bustle of modern life.

The surrounding landscape and the close proximity to the river, parks, tourist area, harbor and shopping area that make this a prime location for the hotel business.

Recognization as (sample: UNESCO World Heritage Site)

The hotel is situated in the *(which city/town)* that was Recognization **as (list down the recognition, example: UNESCO World Heritage Site Since 7 July 2008, which is a thriving tourist and business traveler destination).** We are confident that, as the city continues to expand and our hotel will become an established part of this popular destination.

Premises

- **Write down your premise address and the offer that your provide.**

Parking

Parking facilities will be our own parking lot for cars to accommodate a 18 to 20 lot for staff and customer. **(write your own parking lot here if any)**

Security

The hotel will be outfitted with a state of the art security system in addition to smoke alarms ad a sprinkler system. This will include a CCTV (closed circuit television) system for surveillance of al public areas such as the hotel entrance, parking lot, the conference and meeting rooms, and the swimming pool, as well as all corridors, elevators, mini shop, cafe, restaurant and service areas of the hotel. Professionally trained security personnel are part of the hotel staff and can be hired from local security firm to expand any group of visitors' needs.

Cooperation with the local authorities furthermore ensures safe transport to and from **(your hotel to the airport)** Airport whenever this is required. This will ensure that our high profile visitors, be it dignitaries or businessmen, can be assured of safe and secure stay at *Your Company*.

(You can add-in and modify using your own word that is more valuable or suitable to your business)

VI.   Advertising and promotion

Your Company's promotional plan is diverse and includes a range of marketing communications. We will have a Grand Opening to be scheduled upon construction completion which will be advertised in local newspapers and local radio channels. To support expansion efforts, the local considers using popular media, such as local TV, radio, newspapers and the internet to advertise.

It appears that the most successful hotels or resorts spend a percentage of net sales revenue for promotion and advertising. *Your Company* Plans to do likewise with a portion of net sales on a yearly basis. Based on this decision, advertising ad promotional possibilities were prioritized in order of probable effectiveness.

Opening – we will send out an introductory press kit to all media and place printed announcements in key publications.

Ongoing – during the initial year, we intend to get our leaflets displayed in the many venues in the city. The staff will be trained as to promote by word-of-mounth.

Future – for our conference services, we intend to hire a sales representative who will be charge of prospecting for new clients.

Public relations

Press releases are issued to both trade journals and publications such as local and regional newspapers, travel agents, hotel and accommodation magazines, online hotel and restaurant directories and in deal with local Chambers of Commerce.

Analysis of the advertising expenditures / advertising with promotion goals:

These areas will be established with a professional marketing consultant as construction begins. This will allow *Your Company* to prepare for the grand opening and on-going business.

VII.   **SWOT analysis**

Our analysis is based on input collected during discussions with staff, distributors, customers and industry interviews.

Summary of Strengths and Weaknesses

Descriptions	Strengths	Weaknesses
Business climate	Present Effective cost for construction.	An overcapacity in the industry has resulted in a deterioration of trading conditions. Atrophy in consumer spending is fueling decreased visits or numbers.
Internal organization	Built with little (if any) debt load.	Establishment of new organization process will require intense oversight.
Political factors	Strong push for job creation.	Low consumer experience. Increase living costs.
Social factors	Many people spend thier vacations in our region.	Poor economic times are decreasing unnecessary spending.
Workforce	Increase unemployment figures will provide optimal opportunity for full staff.	Internships for unemployed/under-employed workers will require increased number of regular staff.
Economic	High demand due to increasing of visitor/tourist to **your hotel**	Due to overcapacity in the sector profit margins are squeezed to the minimum.

Chart 7: SWOT – Sample of Analysis for Summary of Strengths and Weaknesses

Problems and Possibilities

Descriptions	Problems / Threats	Possibilities / Opportunities
Economic	In times of recession less people may be inclined to travel.	Offer excellent value for money.
Internal organization	Changing of leadership	Establish Board of Directors with community members.
External factors	Lack of community support	Job creation and skills training brings hope and economic uplift to community.
Personnel	Finding qualified personnel can be tedious task.	Motivate current personnel.
Accommodation Mix Price Quality Purchasing Customers Competitors other	Many hotels in area of similar room numbers and pricing.	Emphase focus on business sector and conference space availability
Food Mix Price Quality Purchasing Customers Competitors other	Several restaurant on site	Specific catering for conference needs, complimentary breakfast and room service available (grill).
Conference / Meeting room Mix Price Quality Purchasing Customers Competitors other	Need for increased staff and marketing, increased risk management issues.	No other similar sized space available in area that equip with pricing.
Mini Shop	Nearby shop	In the hotel, competitive price

Chart 8: SWOT – Sample for Analysis for Summary of Strengths and Weaknesses

4.   Learn How To Plan Your Organization Structure

A. Management and personnel: Sample Organization Chart

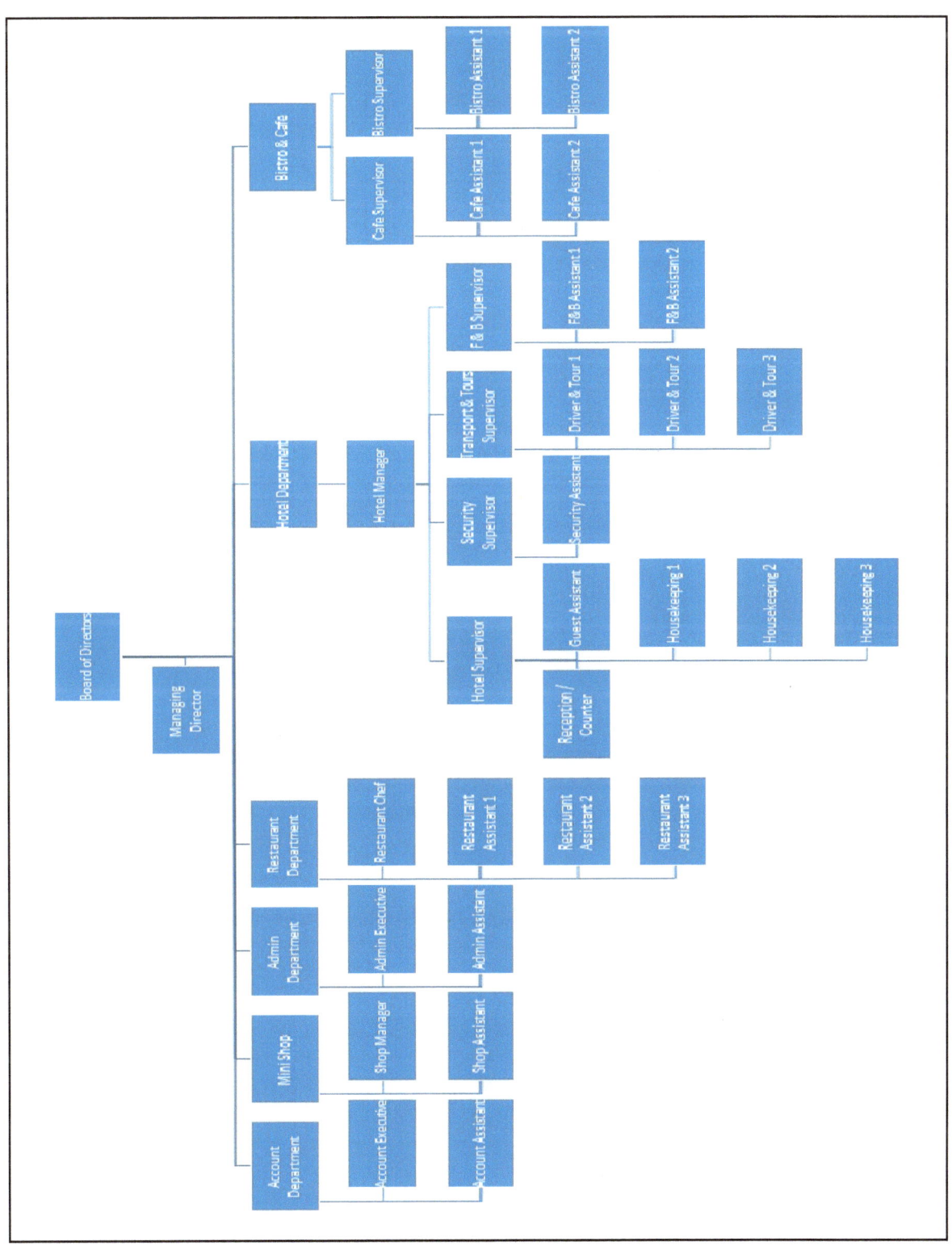

B. Job Descriptions / Work Details (Sample)

❖ ACCOUNT EXECUTIVE
The job role of an Account Executive is to be responsible of looking at the company's client as well as keeping the company's-client relationships at a high standard.
The role of an account executive includes being familiar with the totality of the company's service and knowing all the products as well as having the ability to make a sale without any problems.

❖ ACCOUNT ASSISTANT
Accounts Assistant is responsible for maintaining the accuracy while updating the accounts, payable and receivable sub-ledgers should be checked by the assistant.
Accommodate monthly account with the help of industry specified computer software and in accordance with government policies.

❖ SHOP MANAGER
Completes store operational requirements by scheduling and assigning employees; following up on work results.
Maintains store staff by recruiting, selecting, orienting, and training employees.
Maintains store staff job results by coaching, counselling, and disciplining employees; planning, monitoring, and appraising job results.

❖ SHOP ASSISTANT
Serving customers and taking payments are the key responsibilities of shop assistants. Depending on the retailer worked for, they may also advise customers, assist in locating requested goods, provide information on products, stack and display merchandise, and order stock.
Qualities looked for by employers include trustworthiness, diplomacy and politeness, as well as excellent communication and customer service skills. Candidates should also have a high level of stamina to cope with the long hours and challenging nature of the job.

❖ ADMIN EXECUTIVE
Perform administrative duties for executive management. Responsibilities may include screening calls; managing calendars; making travel, meeting and event arrangements; preparing reports and financial data; training and supervising other support staff; and customer relations. Require strong computer and Internet research skills, flexibility, excellent interpersonal skills, project coordination experience, and the ability to work well with all levels of internal management and staff, outside clients and vendors. Sensitivity to confidential matters may be required.

❖ ADMIN ASSISTANT
Performs administrative and office support activities for multiple supervisors. Duties may include fielding telephone calls, receiving and directing visitors, word processing, creating spreadsheets and presentations, and filing.

Extensive software skills, Internet research abilities and strong communication skills are required. Staff in this category may also have the title of department assistant, coordinator or associate.

❖ RESTAURANT CHEF
Direct the preparation, seasoning, and cooking of salads, soups, fish, meats, vegetables, desserts, or other foods. Plan and price menu items, orders supply, and keep records and accounts. Supervises and participate in cooking and baking and the preparation of foods. Write weekly schedules according to business and projected goals for labour percentages.

❖ RESTAURANT ASSISTANT
Provide excellent services to customers at a restaurant.
Greet restaurant customers in a courteous manner.
Assist and support restaurant chefs in preparing dishes and beverages.
Take orders and serve the customers.
Assist in serving quality food and beverages.

❖ HOTEL MANAGER
The hotel manager provides overall leadership, guidance, and direction to the hotel management team as it strives to provide the highest quality in standards and services.
In addition, this individual acts as the main liaison between the client and hotel staff.
The hotel manager also ensures that hotel and client financial obligations are met.

❖ HOTEL SUPERVISOR
The supervisor also assists the front office team in making reservations and answers incoming telephone calls. Other duties include assisting guests with special requests. When the front desk manager takes a break or is out for the day, the supervisor can generally assist guests as the manager on duty.

❖ RECEPTION / SERVIE COUNTER
A receptionist is an employee taking an office/administrative support position. The work is usually performed in a waiting area such as a lobby or front office desk of an organization or business. The title "receptionist" is attributed to the person who is employed by an organization to receive or greet any visitors, patients, or clients and answer telephone calls.

❖ GUEST ASSISTANT
Guest service assistant is to answer telephone call from guest seeking to make or cancel hotel reservations. They greet arriving guests; assign rooms, issue keys, and collect guest payment and billing information. Agents answer guest requests for assistance and coordinate with housekeeping, bell service, staff and management to fulfil guest requirements.
They provide guests with access to hotel services, forward in-room meal requests, and ensure that mail, faxes and packages are delivered in a timely manner.
They also deal with irate guests and find ways to resolve issues to the guest's satisfaction.

They may also serve as concierges, assisting guests with ground transportation, restaurant or entertainment reservations, and providing other information about the locale.

- ❖ HOUSKEEPING
  Housekeepers are employed either in a private home or in a commercial environment such as a hotel. Duties will vary according to the employment environment but the basic tasks and skills required to perform the housekeeping job remain the same.
  The sample housekeeper job description lists these common tasks and requirements and also identifies the additional tasks and skills required for a housekeeping job in a domestic environment and in a commercial service.

- ❖ SECURITY SUPERVISOR
  The Security Supervisor is responsible for protecting all Company employees and property and providing customers who visit the Company facility with the information they require.
  The Supervisor is also responsible for the supervision of all Company Security Guards, the cleanliness of the guardhouse and the sale and account for public pay phone cards.
  In order to carry out these responsibilities, the Security Supervisor conducts regular checks and foot patrols, verbally helps, directs and interacts with customers and manages the human resources of the Security staff.

- ❖ SECURITY ASSISTANT
  Perform responsible protective service work to maintain and ensure the security of the customer, staff and hotel property while adhering to established rules and regulations; conduct surveillance of hotel buildings, grounds and activities.

- ❖ TRANSPORT & TOURS SUPERVISOR
  You would be responsible for managing the travel arrangements of holiday makers and business clients, making sure everything runs according to plan. To be a good tour manager, you would need experience of planning and organising trips, excellent 'people' skills and foreign. Personal qualities are often more important than formal qualifications.

- ❖ DRIVER TOURS
  Responsible for transporting people from one place to another place and ensures passengers get out safely. Transport passengers on chartered trips or sightseeing tours.
  Drive through traffic and obey traffic laws.
  Stop frequently, often only a few blocks apart and when a passenger requests a stop.
  Answer questions about schedules and routes.
- ❖ F & B SUPERVISOR
  Food and beverage supervisors are responsible for the daily operations of businesses that prepare and serve food and drinks to customers such as restaurants, resorts, hotels, hospitals and banquet halls.

Food and beverage supervisors oversee all of the issues pertaining to a patron's dining experience, such as quality control, staff management, inventory, health and safety regulations and customer service.

❖ F & B ASSISTANT
Responsible to assist in food and beverage operation
Ensure all customers are provided with outstanding service.
Ensure kitchen, restaurant, and bar operations are opened and closed according to policy.
Responsible for ordering supplies, and inventory control and establishing relationship with suppliers ensuring the business receives competitive terms.
Responsible for food hygiene, and health and safety issues
Responsible to assist in menu planning, development and meal specials
Ensure all kitchens and eating areas are organized and maintain a high level of cleanliness
Provides leadership and guidance to all team members
Ensure proper cash management controls are followed by all food & beverage staff members, as per policy.

❖ CAFÉ ASSISTANT
Keeping accurate time sheets daily assisting with ordering supplies, locally where possible
Checking that orders have been correctly delivered and charged for serving customers in a pleasant and courteous manner.
Cleaning the kitchen, café area and café toilets in accordance with Health and Safety Regulations and Guidance
Keeping cleaning and temperature records
Undertaking the preparation of the food and beverages served in the café.
Clearing tables
Washing up
Operating the wood burning stove

❖ BISTRO SUPERVISOR
Assist with restaurant management operations – including supervising, training and leading others.
Handle function enquiries and bookings as well as providing hands on assistance for function events.
Uphold a high level of Spirit Hotel customer service standards across the team.
Provide hotel leadership which enables and develops team members to achieve.
Develop collaborative relationships with department supervisors, kitchen staff and management to provide quality food and prompt service to our customers.

❖ BISTRO ASSISTANT
Make sure employees perform a variety of tasks, from preparing the food, stocking supplies, serving, charging people for their food, handling cash, credit cards, and a cash register, cleaning tables and counters, resetting tables, greeting customers and answering questions.

5. Learn How To Do Your Business Workflow

A. Sample of Hotel Reservation - Offline / Walk-in Workflow

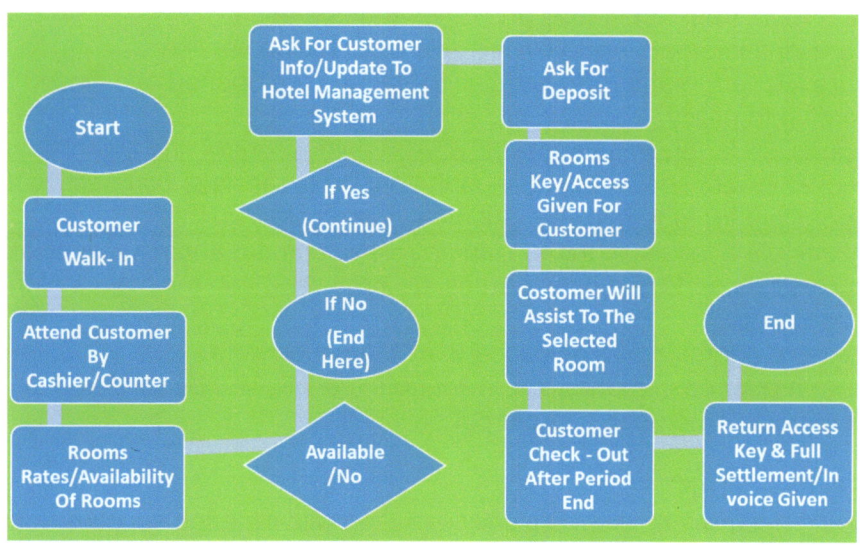

B. Sample Hotel Reservation - Online Workflow

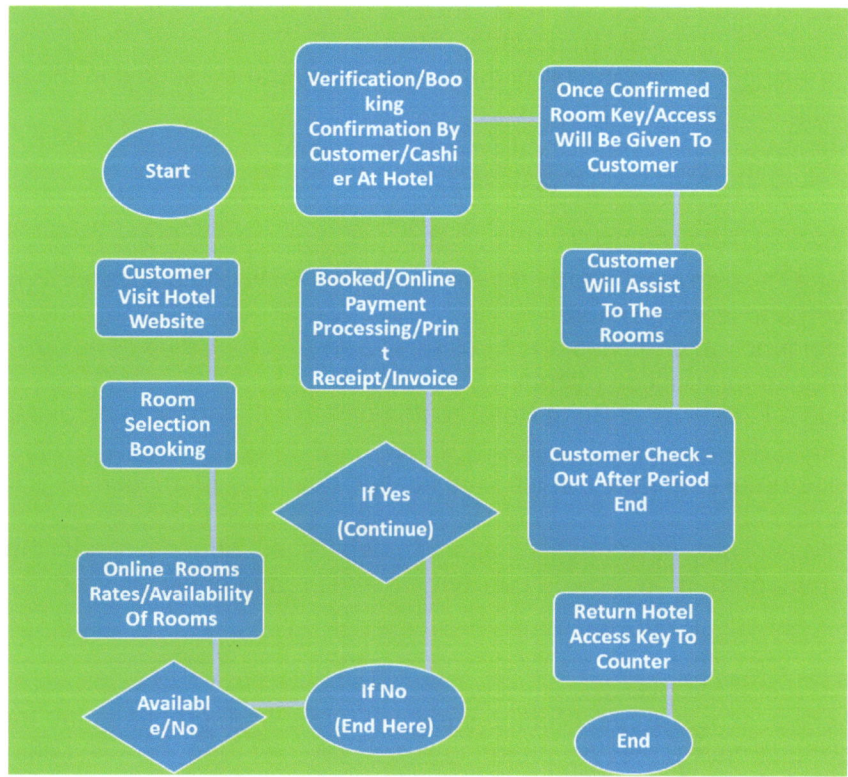

C. Sample Mini Shop Business Workflow (if any)

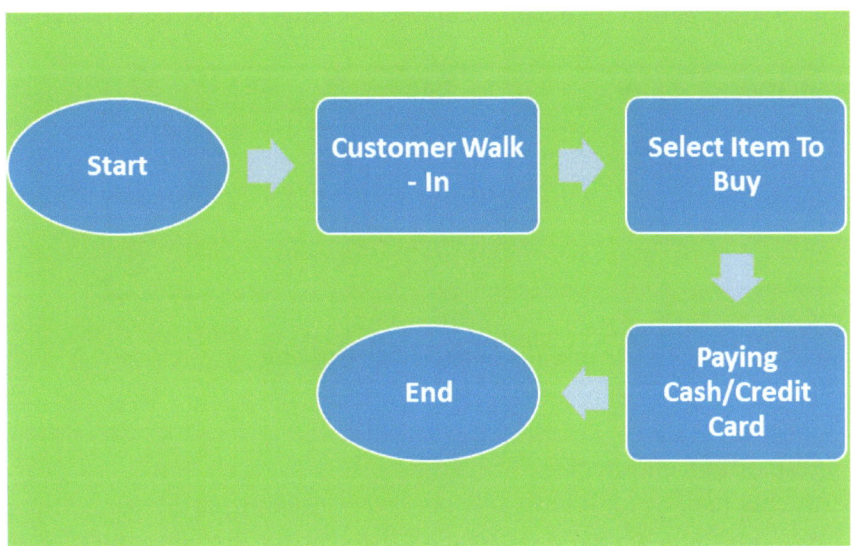

D. Sample Restaurant Business Workflow

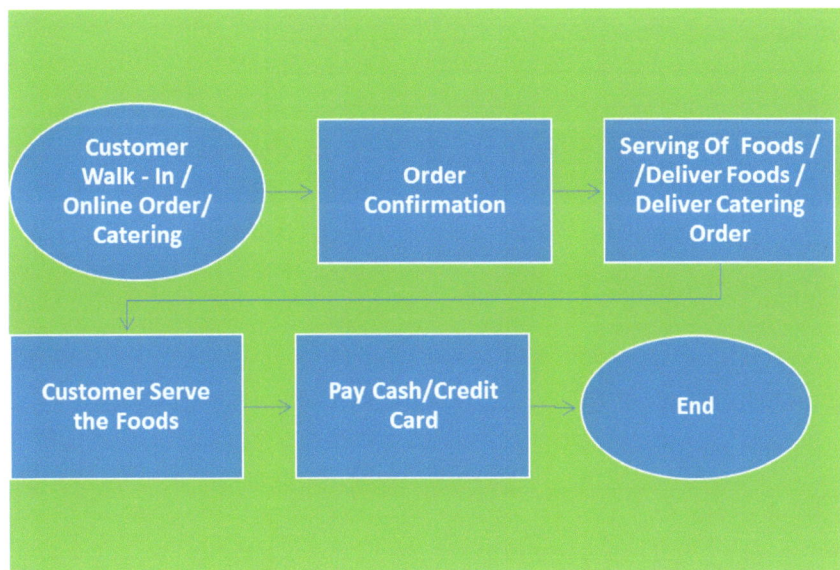

6. **How To Do Project Costing**

    A. Manpower Cost / Staffing Cost
- List down all the position by department and the salary rates, benefit and etc.

No.	Department Salary		Allowance	Others
1	Manager	USD10,000.00	USD350.00	USD100.00

Sample for Manpower Costing

    B. Asset Costing for All Department.
- All departments may need to have like computer / laptop, projector, table, chair, printer, air-condition and etc. List down all the cost for the department asset.

No.	Department	Asset Descriptions	Qtty	Cost/Unit	Total Amount
1	CEO	Computer	1	$2,500.00	$2,500.00
				Total Amount	

Sample of Departmental Asset Costing

7. **Sample Financial Statement & Financing**

    I.   Project Implementation Cost

    II.   Cashflow for the 1st 12 months

    III.   Cashflow for 5 years

    IV.   Profit & Loss for Year 1

    V.   Profit & Loss for 5 Years

    VI.   Balance Sheet

    VII.   Loan Repayment Schedule

    VIII.   Depreciation List for Asset

(This part will be continue in the next edition)

8. **Sample Project Evaluation**

(This part will be continue in the next edition)

9. **Look for Contractor & Architect Background**

- **This part, you can request from your appointed contractor**

10. **Appendix / Other Information**

- Put in all related document / appendix in this part.

THANK YOU

- END –

www.ingramcontent.com/pod-product-compliance
Lightning Source LLC
Chambersburg PA
CBHW041319180526
45172CB00004B/1159